THE ART OF
WINNIE-THE-POOH

THE ART OF
WINNIE·THE·POOH

HOW E. H. SHEPARD
ILLUSTRATED AN ICON

Written by

James Campbell

Foreword by

Minette Shepard

First published in Great Britain in 2017
by LOM Art, an imprint of
Michael O'Mara Books Limited
9 Lion Yard
Tremadoc Road
London SW4 7NQ

A CIP catalogue record for this book is available from the British Library.

Papers used by Michael O'Mara Books Limited are natural, recyclable products
made from wood grown in sustainable forests. The manufacturing processes conform
to the environmental regulations of the country of origin.

ISBN: 978-1-910552-77-3 in hardback print format
ISBN: 978-1-910552-78-0 in ebook format

2 3 4 5 6 7 8 9 10

www.mombooks.com

Cover design by Patrick Knowles
Interior design by Ana Bjezancevic
Typeset by Jade Wheaton

Printed and bound in China.

For Arabee

Ernest Shepard and his great-granddaughter, Arabella Hunt, in 1963.

Contents

Foreword

By Minette Hunt (née Shepard)

I was delighted by the positive reaction to the collection of my grandfather E. H. Shepard's work undertaken during the First World War – *Shepard's War* – and this encouraged us to look again at the extensive archives left by E. H. Shepard to see if these could tell a further story about his most famous drawings: those for Winnie-the-Pooh and the other animals of the Hundred Acre Wood.

Although the drawings for Winnie-the-Pooh are so well known across the world, perhaps less well known is how these actually came about, and the way in which my grandfather worked collaboratively and increasingly closely with A. A. Milne to create these now iconic illustrations. The sketches, drawings and illustrations in this book throw new light on the creative processes which brought about these much-loved depictions of the imaginary toys and animals belonging to Christopher Robin.

The Winnie-the-Pooh books were, unusually for that time, very much a joint venture between Milne and my grandfather. At that time it was usual practice for a publisher to commission an illustrator once a book was written, and the illustrations would be inserted in sections through the book, not necessarily adjacent to relevant text. However, after the great success of *When We Were Very Young*, both Alan Milne and my grandfather realised that they could achieve much more by working closely together to create a seamless experience for the reader. Establishing a joint creative process, they would meet regularly, often weekly, and discuss their respective contributions, making suggestions, proposing alterations and amendments, and often considering the look of the layouts on the printed page, which was extremely unusual. Therefore these books were amongst the first where the illustrations were not an afterthought and distributed randomly through the text, but were an integral part of the story.

Minette Shepard, *c.* 1943.

Throughout this period my grandfather brought to all of his work a great sense of humility and humanity, I suspect partly at least as a result of his experiences in the First World War, and the recollection of his own happy family life when his own children were small probably conjured up something of the childhood innocence of Winnie-the-Pooh. He retained an essential humour, honesty and truthfulness in his artistic work that characterised his approach to life as well as to work. I feel a special and personal connection to my grandfather when I look back over these wonderful drawings which have meant so much to so many childhoods across the world. I had the enormous privilege (not that I realised it at the time) to have had Growler, the model for the drawings of Winnie-the-Pooh, for the very early part of my childhood. I very much hope you will enjoy looking at these illustrations, drawings and photographs, and reading about how they came about, as much as I have done in rediscovering them.

Minette Hunt (née Shepard)
Sussex 2017

Preface

Winnie-the-Pooh, or just Pooh Bear – these words have a unique resonance in our cultural heritage. Across the world, from Tokyo to Los Angeles and from Melbourne to Copenhagen, a picture of Pooh will bring instant recognition, and often a smile.

E. H. Shepard is one of a small and select group of illustrators to remain a household name – even forty years after his death, and more than ninety years after the publication of some of the most famous books of all time. When asked to close one's eyes and conjure up an image of Pooh, what do we see? Inevitably, our personal favourite of E. H. Shepard's evocative and iconic drawings. While the four books – *When We Were Very Young*, *Winnie-the-Pooh*, *Now We Are Six* and *The House at Pooh Corner*, known collectively as the Winnie-the-Pooh books – have never been out of print, and have been through countless editions, the story of how the illustrations of this funny old bear and his friends came about has been relatively little told.

This book tells that story, setting out how between them A. A. Milne and E. H. Shepard created a marriage of stories and pictures that lies at the heart of the timeless attraction of Winnie-the-Pooh. Featuring many previously unseen drawings, sketches and unused illustrations, principally held in archives at the University of Surrey, the Shepard family archive and private collections, this book shows how the images of Pooh and other well-known characters evolved and developed.

E. H. Shepard is principally remembered for his iconic children's illustrations (or 'decorations' as they are always described in the Winnie-the-Pooh books) for the four Pooh books and for *The Wind in the Willows* – all of which were completed within a ten-year period from the early 1920s.

Yet Shepard was much more than just an illustrator of children's books. A prolific artist as well as an illustrator, his first works date from his childhood in the 1880s and he was still drawing in the 1970s – an amazing ten decades of active work across a wide range of subjects and genres. Many feel that Shepard brought much personal experience to the 'decorations' for the Pooh

An early sketch of an anxious looking Winnie-the-Pooh struggling into his duffle coat.

stories, not only in the use of his own son's teddy bear, Growler, as the model for Winnie-the-Pooh, but also in the images of charm, innocence and even whimsy that deliberately harked back to an idealised Edwardian heyday, when Shepard's own children were the age of Christopher Robin. Unusually for that time, he was a very hands-on father, playing make-believe and delving into the dressing-up box to join in their games.

The trauma of the First World War, experienced at first hand by both Milne and Shepard, and the peacetime challenges that immediately followed – the epidemic of Spanish flu, widespread unemployment and other social issues – may have seemed at times overwhelming, and so the Winnie-the-Pooh stories and the way in which they were presented struck a strong chord with families, adults and children alike, desperate for an escape into a comforting fantasy.

And while the stories and poems, largely set in London and in the Ashdown Forest in Sussex, are quintessentially 'English', from the very start they broke free of their natural constraints, selling not only in English-speaking territories, but also in multiple languages (including Latin) across the world. In all of these editions, languages and countries, one thing remains absolutely consistent: the 'decorations'. Shepard's drawings have universal appeal, need no translation and have an enduring resonance with adults and children of all ages.

While Milne wrote no more about Pooh and his friends after 1928, Shepard continued to draw, colour and illustrate new editions of the original four books until shortly before his death in 1976, at the age of ninety-six. In this book you will find sketches, outlines and drafts that have never before been shown, and which throw a new light on the creative process that brought Winnie-the-Pooh to life. Shepard never tired of 'the bear', always aware of the reach and connection of the characters and their images around the world. In this century, Shepard would almost certainly have been amazed to see both the Winnie-the-Pooh books and *The Wind in the Willows* consistently in the top ten of children's literature. He was a very modest genius.

CHAPTER 1

Shepard and Milne: The Early Years

Ernest Howard Shepard was born on 10 December 1879 in London, the third and youngest child of Henry Shepard, an architect, and his wife, Jessie Lee. When Shepard was born the family were living in Springfield Road, St John's Wood, but shortly afterwards moved to Kent Terrace, near Regent's Park. It was a comfortable, middle-class environment, with both parents coming from professional backgrounds with artistic and literary connections.

Shepard's childhood sketch of Hussars relaxing while on exercise near Aldershot.

Henry Shepard's family were well-to-do, his father being a successful property developer and builder, who had built the substantial corner house in Gordon Square, Bloomsbury, in which he lived with his large family, including Henry's unmarried sisters. After the death of their parents, four of his sisters continued to live in comfort in Gordon Square, and regularly invited the Shepard children to join them on their summer holidays, when they would take a house in the 'country'. At first, as the aunts were anxious about the safety of trains (a new innovation of the time), the 'country' was often only as far as Wimbledon or Highgate, effectively suburbs of London; but as their anxiety over trains diminished, they became bolder and the children were able to have happy holidays in rented houses in the home counties and even as far afield as Hampshire. Shepard was fascinated from a young age by army and military matters, and on one occasion followed a group of Hussars on an exercise from Aldershot, capturing them relaxing by the roadside in an early sketch.

Shepard's childhood was in many ways an idyllic one – he probably saw more of his parents, and certainly of his mother, than most of his contemporaries; he seems to have got on well with his siblings, Ethel and Cyril; and he even formed affectionate relationships with the domestic staff 'below stairs'. He was encouraged to draw from an early age, and some of his earliest surviving drawings date from the mid-1880s onwards, when he documented some of the key events of the era, including Queen Victoria's Golden Jubilee, the spectacle of the great fire at Whiteleys department store in Bayswater and the royal wedding of Prince George to Princess May of Teck (later King George V and Queen Mary). This charming drawing in pen and ink gives a wonderful impression of the prancing escort of mounted horses, with the royal carriage centre stage and crowds cheering in the streets and from buildings overlooking the route – remarkable work for a thirteen-year-old. Shepard's own memoir, *Drawn from Memory* (published in 1957), gives a wonderful evocation of this happy time.

Shepard, at the age of thirteen, sketched the marriage procession of
Prince George, Duke of York, and Princess May of Teck, London, 1893.

Sadly, however, his mother, Jessie, had become an invalid and died when Shepard was just ten years old, and in many ways this marked the end of his blissful and uncomplicated childhood. Henry Shepard clearly took his wife's death very hard – they seem to have been a devoted couple – and to some extent he appears to have been unable to cope. Ethel, Cyril and Ernest were sent, initially only temporarily, to live with their aunts in Gordon Square, but they ended up staying for nearly a year, and would never return to the house at Kent Terrace. At about this time, and possibly as a result of his wife's death, Henry Shepard's life took a gradual financial downturn, and the family suffered accordingly, with several moves to cheaper accommodation in London. Fortunately, Henry's brother was a teacher at St Paul's School in west London and was able to arrange advantageous terms for the school fees, allowing the boys to attend as day pupils. It was at St Paul's that Ernest's exceptional artistic talents were recognised; the headmaster arranged for him to be in a special drawing class and he was sent to Heatherley's art school on Saturdays for life classes, all with the intention of preparing him for the scholarship examinations to the Royal Academy Schools – at that time one of the most prestigious art schools in London.

(left and opposite)
Pages from a school sketchbook showing Shepard's early gift for figures.

Shepard was successful, winning a scholarship to the RA Schools, and during his time there received further prizes and awards, which gave him some much-needed financial independence and security, as by this time his father's health and finances were sliding further downhill. The family moved to Blackheath, for its clearer air and cheaper accommodation, and Shepard gave up the studio in Chelsea that he had been sharing with a friend in order to join his siblings in caring for their father. Henry died in 1902 at the age of just fifty-six. Ethel never married but became a Church of England missionary and spent considerable time in India, while Cyril took a job as an underwriter in the Lloyd's of London insurance market. Shepard left the

Pencil sketch of Graham Howard Shepard aged about four.

RA Schools as a star pupil, having exhibited regularly and with the honour of having a portrait in oils selected for the Royal Academy Summer Exhibition, which was hung 'on the line' (meaning that it was hung at eye level, a mark of prestige) and sold at a good price, considering he was an unknown artist.

At about this time, Shepard met and fell in love with another student, Florence Chaplin, who was known to family and close friends as Pie. She was four years older than Shepard and came from a very similar background. Sure that she would not be attracted to him, Shepard was nervous about approaching her, but in due course he plucked up the courage to tell her how he really felt, and was amazed when she returned his affections. They decided to get married, although neither had any money, and were certain that Pie's widowed mother would oppose the match on these grounds. Pragmatically, however, she simply asked that Shepard insure his life, and on this basis gave her consent. They were married in 1904 and set up home in a modest cottage in Shamley Green, just south of Guildford in Surrey. They both painted and drew to raise an income, and, at first, Pie was the more successful. Their son, Graham, was born in 1907, and their daughter, Mary, on Christmas Day in 1909, completing the family. This simple pencil sketch (opposite), marked 'G.H.S.' (Graham Howard Shepard), was one of many drawn by Shepard of his son during these years.

This period with his young family was possibly the happiest of Shepard's life. He had a wife he adored and two children on whom he doted, inventing pet names and secret games for them, playing dressing-up and creating a fantasy world where the children's toys and animals were brought to life in wonderful stories. This time, when the children were young and life was carefree and innocent, was very important when Shepard later came to draw Winnie-the-Pooh and the characters conjured up by A. A. Milne. He was able to think back and visualise the games of make-believe played with Graham's teddy bear, Growler, and the children's other toys, and which the whole family had so much enjoyed.

His career as a freelance artist and illustrator progressed during the first decade of the century, but only slowly at first, and the Shepards lived very much hand-to-mouth, as money was tight and there was no other source of family money to fall back on. Shepard regularly sent cartoons, drawings

Mary and Graham Shepard, plus Growler, *c.* 1912.

Early draft for a book dust jacket,
likely from 1900–1910.

and illustrations speculatively to a variety of publications, including *Punch* magazine, and received frequent rejections. But gradually he built up a practice from a portfolio of publishers, principally for periodicals but also for book illustrations. The pencil drawing here (above) of a woodland scene with a crouched figure and blank panels for the publisher's information (book title, author name and so on) would have been typical of the drafts he would submit to publishers, from which he would work up more detailed drawings later on. He worked at home in a small studio in the garden at Shamley Green, and would use a Triumph motorbike to get to Guildford station and commute into London whenever necessary.

Shepard's studio at
Shamley Green, Surrey.

By the outbreak of war in 1914, Shepard had established a solid reputation
as an artist and illustrator, managed to bring in a regular (if not large) income
and the family had been able to move to a larger cottage in the village. Always
keen on military matters, he chafed at not being allowed to volunteer to
fight (as he was both married and too old for the volunteer army) until
1915, when the rules were relaxed and he signed up as an officer in the Royal
Garrison Artillery. As the most junior officer in a field battery, he fought with
distinction on the Western Front, seeing action at the Battle of the Somme
(where his brother, Cyril, was killed on the first day) and at Passchendaele
before being transferred to the Italian front, where he was actively engaged
on the Asiago plain and at Piave. He managed not only to serve with great
courage (being awarded the Military Cross in 1917), but also worked for the
Military Intelligence Services, continued to keep up his civilian illustration
practice and wrote hundreds of letters, mostly to Pie, detailing his experiences.
After being demobbed in the spring of 1919 – by which point he had attained
the rank of Acting Major and was in command of the field battery – he
returned home and resumed his freelance practice, reconnecting swiftly with
a wide range of clients, including *Punch* magazine and the publishing house
Methuen. By the early 1920s he was well established as a creative, innovative
and reliable professional artist and illustrator.

Self-portrait of Shepard in his officer's uniform.

Alan Alexander Milne
and his son Christopher
Robin Milne, *c.*1932.

Alan Alexander Milne was born in 1882 in London, where his father, J. V. Milne, ran a boys' preparatory school in Kilburn. He was the youngest of three brothers, and was particularly close to his elder brother, Ken, just sixteen months his senior. The Milne family were middle class, reasonably well off and well connected within professional London society, via the parents and families of the school's pupils. Notably, the school employed H. G. Wells to teach maths and science, and the future newspaper magnate Alfred Harmsworth was a pupil, who set up the school magazine, to which Milne contributed.

Milne progressed through his father's school with a reputation as the brightest of the three siblings, and so it was little surprise when he won a Queen's Scholarship to Westminster School. Here, however, his academic precocity did not endure, and he seems to have become increasingly disengaged from maths and more interested in literature. Nonetheless, he went up to Trinity College, Cambridge, in 1900 to study mathematics, and by 1902 had become editor of the Cambridge literary magazine *Granta*. The magazine was well connected to other national periodicals, including *Punch*, and so on leaving university Milne moved easily into working as a freelance writer. He submitted work to *Punch* which published his first piece in August

1904. Milne was fortunate that his father was able to support him in a freelance career, unlike Shepard, and he did not have the anxiety of having to be financially self-sufficient.

In 1910 Milne was introduced to his future wife, Dorothy de Sélincourt. It does not seem to have been an immediate attraction, as although they had met socially from time to time, it was not until 1913 that they became engaged to be married, having met once again on a skiing holiday in Switzerland. Dorothy – or Daphne, known usually as Daffs to Milne – was from a rather grander family, and was accustomed to moving in a more elevated social sphere. She brought comfort and stability to his life, acted as adviser and secretary and created an ordered domestic existence in which he could write without distraction.

Milne was not only a writer but also a pacifist – possibly influenced by his former teacher H. G. Wells – but he was persuaded to enlist when permitted in 1915 (like Shepard), mostly in the belief that the First World War really would be the 'war to end all wars', and that thereafter peace and pacifism would prevail. He trained as a Signals Officer and, like Shepard, saw action at the Battle of the Somme and was later invalided home. Through his published work in *Punch*, Milne had a wide readership for his prose and poetry and his work was well regarded. In 1920 the Milnes' only child, Christopher Robin Milne, was born in London, where they lived in Mallord Street, Chelsea. By the early 1920s, therefore, A. A. Milne was married with a young son, comfortably off and with an established literary reputation. Milne saw himself principally as a playwright and poet – and indeed was anxious to be remembered as such – and not as a children's author. When he wrote the poem 'Vespers', which would ultimately be included in *When We Were Very Young*, he did not consider it as intended for children, but had written it principally for private use; in due course Milne gave the poem to his wife as a gift, with the almost throwaway remark that if she were so inclined she could see if anyone would publish it, and if so, she could keep any resulting income. She did decide to have 'Vespers' published. It is not known whether she attempted to do so in Britain, but it was duly published in New York, for the princely sum of $50.

Thus Shepard and Milne shared many similarities: contemporaries in age, they were born and brought up in the same part of London and came from similar backgrounds, each the youngest of three siblings and with a particular talent that was identified and nurtured. They both worked freelance with a connection to *Punch* magazine, both had served as officers in the First World War, and both were married with children. A promising start for a creative collaboration.

CHAPTER 2

The Punch Table

From the mid-Victorian period up until the Second World War it was a golden age for newspapers, magazines and periodicals. It was not until the 1930s that radio became established as a universal medium for communication (and not until the 1950s for television). And so, for the increasing numbers of the wider population interested in news, comment, fiction and entertainment, the written word was paramount. *Blackwood's*, the *Strand* magazine, the *Illustrated London News* and countless other publications responded to this demand, but the pinnacle of the periodical market was firmly held by

Pencil drawing of a central
London street scene enclosed
in an oval panel surrounded
by vignettes of contemporary
London life, likely submitted
to *Punch*.

Punch magazine. It was the hope of every aspiring writer and illustrator to reach the giddy heights of publication in *Punch*, with its enormous circulation and influential readership. Furthermore, there was by the early part of the twentieth century a well-established practice for authors to publish works as chapters or extracts in magazines prior to publication in book form (the novels of Charles Dickens, for example, were initially published in this way). Not only did this drive up readership numbers, it also created demand for the completed book. This practice would cover not only novels, but also social commentary and poetry.

Punch magazine was a weekly institution, read not only by the great and the good (who would also read *The Times*), but by a vast readership much larger than the actual circulation of the magazine, as it was made so widely available – many will remember its presence well into the third quarter of the twentieth century in waiting rooms, from railway stations to dentists. *Punch* combined political comment and caricature with articles about social and contemporary issues, fiction as short stories and instalments of longer works, poetry, puzzles and a range of advertisements. It could be found across the globe: widely in Britain and also throughout the Empire and in English-speaking countries, including North America.

E. H. Shepard already had a number of family and professional connections with *Punch* at the start of his career, but these do not appear to have smoothed his path to gaining success within its distinguished portals. He submitted unsolicited drawings and cartoons periodically from around the time of his marriage in 1904, but with little luck in the beginning, his first successful submission not being published until 1907. Thereafter, he contributed increasingly frequently across a wide range of subjects. The oval pencil drawing of central London surrounded by vignettes of scenes from around the capital (on the previous page) was typical of the style of drawings he submitted at this time, and by the outbreak of the First World War he was a reasonably frequent contributor to the magazine.

In parallel, A. A. Milne's work for *Punch* developed rapidly from 1904 onwards. In 1905 his brother Ken, who was working as a solicitor in London, married, and Milne became very close to his wife, Maud, and their children, particularly their first child, Marjorie. Milne started to write about 'Margery' (*sic*) in pieces in *Punch*, demonstrating an early facility not only to capture the world of a child but also to convey this without over-sentimentality to an adult audience. In 1906, after only two years, he had published over thirty pieces; at the precocious age of twenty-four he was appointed Assistant Editor, and in 1910 received the ultimate accolade of 'signing the *Punch* table'. It was at this table where the principal contributors to *Punch* gathered weekly to agree the editorial position of the magazine, and to decide the subject matter for the principal cartoons for each edition. This tradition saw those elevated to the senior editorial team scoring their initials into the wooden surface of the *Punch* boardroom table.

After the end of the First World War, Milne and Shepard, in their separate ways, re-established professional relationships with *Punch*. Yet Milne's attempted return to his editorial position at the magazine was frustrated. He had understood that when he left *Punch* in 1915 he was essentially taking leave of absence to fight in the war, and that his position as Assistant Editor would be held open for him until his return. However, the Editor, Owen Seaman, was of the opinion that Milne had resigned from his Assistant Editorship upon joining the army and, having made alternative arrangements, Seaman did not want Milne back in his former post. This misunderstanding – or disagreement – probably resulted from Seaman's view that as a pacifist Milne was an unpatriotic radical, and he did not want a person with such views in a management position at the magazine. Milne eventually accepted that he would not return to *Punch* in any editorial capacity, and resolved to focus principally on writing plays and poetry, although he subsequently submitted pieces on a freelance basis.

By 1921 Shepard was a full member of the *Punch* table, an indication of his rising status within the magazine, and an important and influential colleague there was E. V. Lucas, who was not only an author himself, but soon to become the Chairman of the publisher Methuen. The turning point in Shepard's professional life came after a *Punch* dinner in 1923. Shepard was approached by Lucas, and described what happened next in his own words, which can be seen on the following page.

It is not clear at this stage whether the suggestion was for Shepard to illustrate Milne's children's poems in *Punch*, or simply to provide the fifty or so illustrations required for the book that Methuen had contracted to publish. It was also unclear at that stage whether Lucas had Milne's agreement, or if he was merely sounding Shepard out as a possibility.

Genesis of Pooh   written in 1956   1958/59/60 (1) 1500 words

One Wednesday evening late early in the autumn of 1923 1924, I was sitting next to E. V. Lucas at our weekly Punch dinner. Besides being an Author, Lucas was also managing director chairman of Methuen the publishers. He leaned across Turned to me and said, quite casually, "Ernest, we have some charming poems for Children sent to us by A. A. Milne and we want to publish them, would you like to illustrate them?" I said "Yes" without a moment's hesitation for though I did not know Milne (he had given up coming to the Punch Table by that time) of course I was familiar with his writing. That was my introduction to "When we were very Young". I did not have to wait long before the first poems reached me, among them "Teddy Bear" and "The King's Breakfast" and I realised what a grand time was ahead of me. I took some of my first sketches to show Milne It is nervous work making a picture of an author's written words and when I took my first sketches to show Milne, I felt anxious had some anxious moments while he studied them. It was clear that he was pleased and he said They are fine. So right ahead. Then he added "There will be about Fifty altogether You know." Before the book was ready planned to publish a few poems in Punch, with my illustrations. Owen Seaman was the Editor and he had some doubts about the venture and expressed his doubts these to me. "You know, these poems are for Children and seem hardly suitable for the pages of Punch — however, we shall see". The answer was very convincing, as the Grown-ups seemed to be just as pleased with the poems as were the Children. The first Two to appear, with my illustrations, were the "King's Breakfast" and "Teddy bear" and were promptly bought, one by a Naval Officer and the other by an Army officer stationed abroad. The book was published in November October 1924 and achieved immediate success. The first edition sold out within a few days and the book is still running through endless editions both in the United States and in this country. The popularity of these poems for children The publishers wished to follow this up with another book, but Milne was not to be hurried. He told me that he would do so in due course and then added "in any case, I shall want you to illustrate it". So followed, Two years later, Winnie the Pooh — Then, the following

380 220 60

I worked all through the winter and by February I had done my fifty drawings and the book was going to press

'Genesis of Pooh' – Shepard's handwritten notes
from 1956 describing how E. V. Lucas asked him
to illustrate 'some charming poems' by A. A. Milne.

Shepard's involvement was no done deal. Milne's work both in *Punch* and elsewhere had been illustrated by a number of artists, some much better known than Shepard. Milne's first 'children's' book, *Once On a Time*, written in 1915 as Milne was about to go to war but not published until 1917, was illustrated in the first edition by H. M. Brock, and in a subsequent edition in 1922 by Charles Robinson. A. H. Watson was also considered as a potential illustrator, as was A. E. Bestall, who later illustrated another bear, Rupert.

Initially, Milne was not particularly enamoured of the idea of Shepard as illustrator, and in an introduction to a collection of Shepard's drawings in 1927 he explained why:

> *Perhaps this will be a good place in which to tell the story of how I discovered him. It is short, but interesting. In those early days before the war, when he was making his first tentative pictures for* Punch, *I used to say to F. H. Townsend, the Art Editor, on the occasion of each new Shepard drawing, 'What on earth do you see in this man? He's perfectly hopeless,' and Townsend would say complacently, 'You wait.' So I waited. That is the end of the story, which is shorter and less interesting than I thought it was going to be. For it looks now as if the discovery had been somebody else's. Were those early drawings included in this book, we should know definitely whether Townsend was a man of remarkable insight, or whether I was just an ordinary fool. In their absence we may assume fairly safely that he was something of the one and I more than a little of the other. The Shepard you see here is the one for whom I waited; whom, in the end, even I could not fail to recognise.*

There was apparently a rough sketch of an early cartoon by Shepard with the *Punch* Art Editor's scribbled comment 'make 'em recognisable as humans', which may help us understand why Milne, at this early stage, admitted to thinking that Shepard might be 'perfectly hopeless'.

However, Lucas was convinced that Shepard was the man, and the initial sketches and drawings that Shepard produced persuaded Milne that Shepard was indeed the man. Even so, further issues arose as Shepard's designs for the poems to be published in *Punch* deviated from the normal pattern of a separation between text and illustration. The Editor, Owen

Seaman, needed to be convinced that having line drawings interspersed with text and sitting around the text itself was an innovation to be welcomed rather than feared. Fortunately, in this Shepard was supported by F. H. Townsend, *Punch*'s Art Editor at that time, who also helped Shepard to make his illustrations work with the setting of the text, the larger format of *Punch*'s pages (as compared to the later book illustrations) making this contrast between text and drawings even more effective. The drawings themselves were different from Shepard's usual *Punch* cartoons and illustrations – they were less detailed and finished, and retained a freer style and more relaxed imagery that was more in line with his sketches than with many 'finished' drawings. This new approach delighted Milne, Lucas and colleagues at *Punch*, who had perhaps had some lingering doubts about Shepard's ability to bring Milne's poetry to life.

Of particular interest in this initial collection are the illustrations for one of the most famous and popular of the poems, 'The Dormouse and the Doctor'. In 1923 Rose Fyleman, who was editing a children's magazine called *The Merry-Go-Round*, asked Milne for some verse suitable for children. He responded by sending her 'The Dormouse and the Doctor', which was first illustrated by Harry Rountree. We can therefore compare the two illustrators' approaches to exactly the same text. Rountree had envisaged both the Doctor and the Dormouse as rodents, and had the very bewhiskered Doctor in striped trousers and tailcoat. His drawings are detailed in a style similar to early Disney cartoons; for example, there is more than a passing resemblance between Rountree's Doctor and Mickey Mouse. Shepard, however, treats the protagonists of the poem within a human context, showing the Doctor, again with striped trousers, frock coat and top hat, as a contemporary London doctor would have appeared at that time, while the Dormouse is shown as a rather charming rodent, more like a dormouse, in fact. The other human characters in the illustrations, including a children's nurse (who looks very similar to the nurse in 'Buckingham Palace') and a chauffeur, are drawn in a contemporary style.

E. V. Lucas was so pleased by the impact of Shepard's illustrations in *Punch* that he commissioned him to illustrate his own forthcoming book of verse, *Playtime and Company*, and Eva Erleigh's *The Little One's Log*. Indeed, Methuen was to commission a great deal of work from Shepard

THE MERRY-GO-ROUND

2

THE DORMOUSE AND THE DOCTOR
BY A. A. MILNE

THERE once was a Dormouse who lived in a Bed
Of delphiniums [blue] and geraniums [red],
And all the day long he'd a wonderful view
Of geraniums [red] and delphiniums [blue].

A Doctor came hurrying round, and he said,
' Tut-tut, I am sorry to find you in bed :
Just say " Ninety-nine," while I look at your chest. . . .
Don't you find that chrysanthemums answer the best ? '

The Dormouse looked round at the view and replied
[When he'd said ' Ninety-nine '] that he'd tried and he'd tried,
And much the most answering things that he knew
Were geraniums [red] and delphiniums [blue].

Harry Rountree's initial illustrations for 'The Dormouse and the Doctor'.

The Dormouse and the Doctor

There once was a Dormouse who lived in a bed
Of delphiniums (blue) and geraniums (red),
And all the day long he'd a wonderful view
Of geraniums (red) and delphiniums (blue).

Shepard's later illustrations for the same poem.

Shepard's colour drawing for the dust jacket
of Eva Erleigh's *The Little Ones' Log*.

Pencil sketch for 'Spring!' in London, possibly
intended for *Punch* – undated, but probably 1920s.

from this time onwards. Shepard also continued to draw for *Punch*, often with a focus on London, and London scenes would go on to be a recurring theme in Milne's two books of poetry *When We Were Very Young* and *Now We Are Six*.

CHAPTER 3

When We Were Very Young

The response to the publication of the initial selection of Milne's poems with Shepard's illustrations in *Punch* was overwhelmingly enthusiastic, and E. V. Lucas accelerated plans for the publication of a full anthology of Milne's verse for children – or, as Milne himself put it: 'They are a curious collection; some for children, some about children, some by, with or from children.' Given the positive response from critics and the public alike to both the poems and the illustrations, there was no question from this point onwards whether Shepard would continue to illustrate the verses.

Shepard estimated that about fifty drawings would be necessary for *When We Were Very Young* and, as usual, he cast his mind about for models. But how did Shepard work? We know that he drew and sketched incessantly, and he himself regularly remarked that there was rarely a day when he did not draw something of interest. He generally carried a small sketchbook and pencil with him in order to quickly record things he found of interest, and a number of these small sketchbooks still exist, attesting to Shepard's ability to capture a scene with just a few lines. He would often then use these quick sketches to work up more detailed drawings in larger drawing books, which were sometimes focused on a particular project – a new book, for example.

The poems mostly feature Christopher Robin in some guise, and many others are longer poems that started out as stories told to Christopher Robin by his father. Most of them had been written – and some published – from 1921 onwards. Shepard's starting point was his illustrations for the original eleven poems commissioned by *Punch*, but these needed to be adapted for the smaller page layout of the book. Shepard and Milne worked together to ensure the layouts were altered as little as possible, although that wasn't always practical. A good example of this was the illustration for the poem 'The King's Breakfast': the poem had been reproduced across a full page of *Punch*, with the illustrations circling around the text; in the published book, the illustrations were instead broken up and linked with relevant passages. It is worth noting that due to the smaller format of the book it was often impossible to replicate the original layout and occasionally some illustrations had to be omitted entirely. 'Lines and Squares' was a good example of this, where the final drawing in *Punch*, of the bear eating up someone who had stepped on a line on the pavement, was left out of the book (although this might have in part been because such a gory ending was rather at odds with the rest of the poems).

Shepard used illustrations to link poems, with similar images throughout enhancing the impression of connection across the anthology. The King and Queen in 'Disobedience' (perhaps better known as James James Morrison Morrison) are almost identical to those in 'The King's Breakfast'; the Doctor in 'Rice Pudding' looks as though he has just come from treating the Dormouse; and, of course, Christopher Robin himself

A page from one of Shepard's many sketchbooks, showing
at the top the gnarled branch of a tree and below a series of
figures of country people. These drafts would be used for the
two books of poems, for example, in 'Jonathan Jo'.

THE KING'S BREAKFAST

The King asked
The Queen, and
The Queen asked
The Dairymaid:
'Could we have some butter for
The Royal slice of bread?'
The Queen asked
The Dairymaid,
The Dairymaid
Said, 'Certainly,
I'll go and tell
The cow
Now
Before she goes to bed.'

The Dairymaid
She curtsied,

And went and told
The Alderney:
'Don't forget the butter for
The Royal slice of bread.'

The Alderney
Said sleepily:
'You'd better tell
His Majesty
That many people nowadays
Like marmalade
Instead.'

An example of how the layout for the
'The King's Breakfast' was adapted for
the smaller pages of the book.

runs as a theme through many of the poems. There are great similarities in the figures of the small boy and small girl throughout, and whereas A. A. Milne was probably thinking principally of his own son, Christopher Robin, Shepard was possibly casting his mind back to the childhoods of his own two children, Graham and Mary, in that Edwardian summer before the First World War.

Christopher Robin Milne and Anne Darlington at Cotchford Farm in 1924, with Shepard's description on the reverse.

Shepard's usual practice was to produce a number of variations for Methuen and Milne to consider. For instance, at this time, Shepard sketched a number of drawings of fashionable women, possibly as models for the mother in the poem 'Disobedience'; later on, Shepard would create further sketches, updating the dress of the mother in line with contemporary fashion. He would then bring the chosen elements together in more worked-up drawings, often taking an element drawn in pencil, turning it over and covering the reverse of the paper in pencil or graphite in order to trace it on to a larger ensemble, as can be seen in the image of James James Morrison Morrison on his tricycle in 'Disobedience' (opposite).

This pencil drawing of a fashionable lady of the early 1920s could easily have been Daphne Milne, but was almost certainly an inspiration for the mother in the poem 'Disobedience'.

Shepard's drawing for a later coloured edition of
'Disobedience' shows the mother in a shorter and
more contemporary dress (*above*). The published
illustration is shown below.

The shorter poems generally only needed one illustration, with perhaps an additional vignette to insert in a suitable position, depending on the typesetting. Longer poems were discussed between Milne and Shepard to see where drawings might enhance the story and provide punctuation points. Often, illustrations were used in order to break up the page, so that the reader and listener were not faced with an intimidating amount of text and could always be looking forward to the next pause at an appropriate drawing.

Winnie-the-Pooh makes his first appearance in 'Teddy Bear', originally published as a single poem on 13 February 1924 in *Punch*. The poem features a bear called Teddy Bear – but no mention is made of the name Winnie-the-Pooh. Moreover, it's important to remember that Teddy Bear made barely an appearance in *When We Were Very Young*, and there was no mention of any of the other animals of the Hundred Acre Wood. Indeed, the bear made only a fleeting appearance in just three of the poems in this first collection of verse. He first shows up three-quarters of the way through the book, in the poem 'Halfway Down' and only in illustrated form. The poem itself describes Christopher Robin sitting halfway down the stairs and thinking aloud about being neither up nor down – but nowhere is there any mention of a bear, or indeed any toy. Yet there, in Shepard's iconic illustration, lie a number of toy animals on the top step, most prominent of which, lying on his side, head slightly over the edge of the step and one leg in the air, is, without any shadow of a doubt, a very familiar bear. But why is the bear there? We know that Christopher Robin's favourite toy was his bear, and that A. A. Milne had been telling him stories about his teddy bear, and so perhaps it was natural that any selection of Christopher Robin's toy animals should feature the bear in a reasonably prominent position. And without the toys, the picture would appear somewhat austere. But it would be fascinating to know if, at this stage, plans were already made for the bear to take on a more prominent role.

So how would Shepard draw this bear, who would end up being so special? To start with, Shepard drew Christopher Robin's own teddy bear, but both he and Milne agreed that this was not going to work. The bear was too angular and had a rather firm jaw. They needed a bear that was

Published illustration for 'Halfway Down', and the
first view of the bear who would become known
as Winnie-the-Pooh.

A page from a 1920s sketchbook with what
is possibly the first ever sketch of what was to
become a very well-known bear.

less threatening, more cuddly and with a twinkle in his eye. So Shepard returned to his own children's toybox, and to Growler, his son Graham's teddy bear. Writing about this time, Shepard said, 'My son, Graham, had a teddy to which he had been deeply attached as a child and I used this bear as my model.'

On a page of a recently unearthed sketchbook, hidden for nearly a century in Shepard's private archive, we find a few lines of what was almost certainly one of his first attempts at drawing a teddy bear (opposite). In just a few strokes we can see the undoubted form of the Winnie-the-Pooh that we still recognise today.

Christopher Robin's
Pooh bear
(as he began life)
in 1924
E.H. Shepard

Shepard's drawing of Christopher Robin's actual bear, which was deemed unfit as a model for Pooh.

The sketch above is for the colour edition of 'Teddy Bear' in *When We Were Very Young*. It is one of the earliest versions of Winnie-the-Pooh (as he was to become). The final, published version is shown below.

A charming early pencil sketch of the 'plump man with a twinkling eye' who is the first to call the teddy 'Mr Edward Bear' (*above*). The final, published version is shown below.

Pencil sketch of
Graham Shepard
aged six, who was later
used as a model for
Christopher Robin.

Furthermore, the discovery of a tiny scrap of paper torn from a sketch pad contains what must be one of the very earliest complete iterations of Winnie-the-Pooh, drawn as just a few lines of soft pencil, holding what looks like a barrel, which was surely to become a jar of honey (shown on page 39). These earliest drawings have never been published before, and add to our understanding of how Shepard worked in building up characters from just a few lines and simple sketches into what would become finished drawings.

There is some obvious confusion over the name of the bear; in the poem 'Teddy Bear', he is known as such until we are properly introduced towards the end of the poem, when we discover he is a Mr Edward Bear. We now understand that this was the first name given by the Milnes to Christopher Robin's bear, but their frequent visits to London Zoo and increasing attachment to Winnie the black bear (originally from Winnipeg, Canada) caused the Milnes' bear to be renamed 'Winnie', Christopher Robin subsequently adding the rather unusual 'Pooh' (his nickname for a pet swan).

Shepard's first illustration in the poem 'Teddy Bear' shows the bear in a very similar position to that of 'Halfway Down' – lying on his back with legs in the air – and then in the next drawing in the sequence we see for the first time the bear standing up, looking at his own reflection in a large freestanding mirror. The successive illustrations are undeniably Pooh Bear, and he makes his final appearance in this anthology at the end of Christopher Robin's bed in 'Vespers'.

Shepard, when recalling how he drew Christopher Robin, said, 'I also had a number of drawings I had made of Graham as a boy of six and these were very useful when, later on, I came to draw Christopher Robin.' The likeness between these sketches of Graham Shepard and some of the drawings was very close, 'Sand Between the Toes' being a good example.

The working relationship between Milne and Shepard was friendly, harmonious and professional, demonstrated by the unusual mention of

The published illustration for 'Sand Between the Toes'.

An unused sketch for 'The King's Breakfast', showing the
Queen eating her bread and honey, and Winnie-the-Pooh
peeking out from behind a curtain.

Shepard in Milne's introduction, in which he concludes: 'In fact, you might
also say that this book is entirely the unaided work of Christopher Robin,
Hoo, and Mr Shepard, who drew the pictures. They have said "Thank you"
politely to each other several times, and now they say it to you for taking
them into your house. "Thank you so much for asking us. We've come."'

When We Were Very Young was published in book form on 6 November
1924 by Methuen in London, and on 20 November by Dutton in New York,
to almost universal acclaim. In Britain the first impression of 5,140 printed
copies sold out on the day of publication, and within eight weeks Methuen
had printed over 40,000 further copies. This was to the great surprise of
bookshops, which had ordered less than 400 in total prior to publication.
In the USA over 10,000 copies had sold by Christmas that year, and by
April Dutton was on to its twenty-third printing. Both Milne and Shepard
seemed genuinely surprised by the outpouring of positive responses from
critics and the buying public alike. Methuen was even more delighted by

the financial success, and having paid Shepard a flat fee of fifty guineas for all his illustrations, handsomely gave him a further cheque for £100 on publication day. But Milne and Shepard were Englishmen of their time – undemonstrative, reserved, uncomfortable talking about 'success' and themselves – and this remained their underlying approach as their partnership went forward. No doubt the Shepard family's decision that Christmas to put on a performance of Milne's earlier children's play *Once On a Time*, which had parts ideally suited to Shepard's children, Graham and Mary, was one way of extending an understated compliment to Milne.

Shepard's handwritten description of his family's production of *Once On a Time* by A. A. Milne.

CHAPTER 4

Winnie-the-Pooh

The four volumes known collectively as the Winnie-the-Pooh books divide into two books of verse (the first and third), and two books of stories about Pooh Bear and his friends in the Hundred Acre Wood (the second and fourth). At the time of publication, and for some years afterwards, the books of verse – which only included a few poems mentioning Winnie-the-Pooh – were more popular than the Pooh storybooks.

WTP p 59

An early pencil
drawing in which Pooh
is holding a jar of
honey while Piglet digs
the heffalump trap.

After the almost instantaneous success of *When We Were Very Young*,
Methuen, *Punch* and the buying public were clamouring for more. E. V.
Lucas had early on identified the teddy bear, who had featured in just three
of the poems in the first collection, as being a potential focus for a sequel.
Lucas knew that Milne already had some stories about Christopher Robin's
bear, which he had told his son in the nursery, and had a hunch that the
bear had great potential, especially in view of the immense popularity of
the real Winnie in London Zoo. Lucas knew that Milne intended a further
volume of verse (which would become *Now We Are Six*), but he felt that a book
of prose stories featuring this bear would be very well received. Moreover,
he was anxious that it be published with all due speed, so as to cash in on
the enthusiasm for the first volume. Milne had written to Lucas saying, 'I
suspect that what you really want is that "Billy Book" you have been urging

me to write ... Fear not. I will do it yet.' 'Billy' was a reference to Christopher Robin, who was known in his early years as Billy Moon – Moon being his attempt to pronounce Milne. On 24 December 1925, in a story commissioned from Milne by the *Evening News* called 'The Wrong Sort of Bees', the name 'Winnie-the-Pooh' first appeared. However, while Lucas and Methuen were extremely keen for this second book to go ahead, Milne did not intend to be rushed, as he had a number of other projects in hand, but he made it clear to Shepard that he would produce the book 'in due course' and added, 'In any case I shall want you to illustrate it.' Shepard described this in an unpublished draft for his memoirs, written in the 1950s.

On this page from Shepard's notebook (corrected and amended by him), he begins, 'Would you like me to tell you how Winnie the Pooh started.'

At that time, such a collaboration between author and illustrator was relatively unusual. Normal practice was for the publisher to determine the number of illustrations and their format as part of their commercial calculations when considering enhancing the sales potential of a book. Usually, the author would be consulted and sometimes given a veto on the choice of illustrator, but this was almost invariably after the text of the book had been completed. Due to the costs of printing, it was also common for illustrations, drawings or photographs to be separated from the text, and with a caption underneath referring the reader to the relevant page of the narrative. Lucas had seen how successful the combining of text and illustrations had been, not only in *Punch* but also in *When We Were Very Young*, and this reinforced his view that this relatively groundbreaking approach would be one of the keys to the book's success.

Milne also appreciated this, and decided to have Shepard involved at the earliest stages of his own creative process. For Shepard, this was moving a step further than when working on *When We Were Very Young*. Previously, he had been commissioned to illustrate the first eleven poems for *Punch* not only after they had been written, but also after some had already been illustrated by other artists. He had effectively been commissioned by Lucas, as publisher, and, as we have seen, initially Milne had to be convinced. Once the poems were commissioned for book form, Shepard then worked around this format, but his relationship with Milne had always been generally reactive, as he followed instructions as to what was required of him.

Shepard himself wrote in a draft of his memoir his own recollection of how his working relationship with Milne developed during the making of *Winnie-the-Pooh*, and of how the work was 'sheer joy' as Milne had given him a 'free hand', which was, again, highly unusual for a book illustrator.

From now on the working relationship was to be proactive on both sides. While Shepard did virtually all his work in his studio in the garden at his home at Shamley Green, he generally went up to London to show and discuss his work. It seems likely that he met Milne at the offices of Methuen at 36 Essex Street, off the Strand, and on occasion at Milne's London home on Mallord Street in Chelsea, which was almost certainly the setting for the staircase with the red carpet that features in 'Halfway

Down' in *When We Were Very Young*, and as the very first illustration in *Winnie-the-Pooh*. Shepard had, as a young man some twenty years earlier, lived in a studio in Glebe Place, Chelsea (at a rent of £50 per annum), so the area was very familiar to him, and Chelsea was still viewed as the haunt of artists and bohemians.

Shepard's handwritten account of how Pooh developed a character of his own, and how he worked closely with Milne to ensure the backgrounds were as accurate as possible.

John Macrae of the American publisher Dutton later wrote, 'During the process of bringing *Winnie-the-Pooh* into existence, I happened to be present at one of the meetings of Milne and Shepard – Milne sitting on the sofa reading the story, Christopher Robin sitting on the floor playing with the characters, which are now famous in *Winnie-the-Pooh*, and, by his side, on the floor, sat E. H. Shepard making sketches for the illustrations which finally went into the book ...'

The Milnes had also recently acquired a country home, Cotchford Farm near Hartfield, a picturesque village by the Ashdown Forest in Sussex, principally used for weekend visits, which allowed Christopher Robin more space to play outside, with the inviting prospect of the forest immediately to hand. At Milne's suggestion, Shepard made several visits there in 1925 and 1926, driving over from Shamley Green to check the

These two sketches of trees are very typical of Shepard's approach. There are hundreds of similar sketches of trees and landscapes from around the Ashdown Forest, and he used these extensively in creating accurate backgrounds.

scenery and topography as described by Milne, who showed him the specific locations for each story. Shepard's preliminary drawings and sketches show the extraordinary attention to detail that he paid to the supposedly fictitious Hundred Acre Wood, and reveal the beauty of its real-world counterpart, Ashdown Forest's Five Hundred Acre Wood. On one occasion, demonstrating the increased warmth of the Milne–Shepard collaboration, the entire Shepard family was asked over for the day. Graham would have been about eighteen, and Mary fifteen. Graham spent the day playing in the stream with Christopher Robin, who was then five, with a log as a make-believe alligator and making dams and mud pies, presumably while the others were with Alan and Daphne Milne. Christopher Robin struck Mary Shepard as being unused to playing with others older than him, and was perhaps surprised that Graham spent all this time with him.

As the stories of Winnie-the-Pooh progressed, Milne would share them with Methuen and Shepard, and between them they would consider how the text could be typeset on the page, and where illustrations would best be incorporated. Shepard would then come up with a series of rough preliminary sketches as suggestions and with alternatives, and Milne would identify which ones he felt would be appropriate. Then, with Methuen, he would consider the appropriate size, scale, position, and so on, so that Shepard could work up the agreed sketches into working illustrations. Even at this stage, Shepard seems to have been amazed and at times exasperated by the stream of messages, notes, instructions and amendments that flowed from Milne. This was exacerbated when material was needed earlier than usual, due to some of the stories being published in a magazine, the *Royal*,

This drawing, a preliminary for the scene in Chapter 6 where Eeyore receives an empty jar of honey from Pooh, shows how in just a few strokes of the pencil Shepard creates a sense of movement, with Eeyore sniffing at the jar and Pooh looking anxious as it is empty. Is that Piglet on the horizon?

This colour sketch marked 'The Wolery' clearly shows how Shepard drew the background and then 'dropped in' the characters. Here he has drawn a rough image of Pooh in pencil across the colour sketch probably to show Methuen and Milne how it might look.

'It was a special pencil case'

p 155

A pencil sketch (*left*) captioned by Shepard 'It was a special pencil case' – note the resemblance of Pooh to the very earliest sketch. The final published illustration is shown below.

A preliminary sketch that wasn't used for the final book,
showing Pooh wading through the flood waters.

prior to book publication. Further, Methuen wanted two stories with
accompanying finished illustrations earlier than planned, so their sales
representatives could show them to bookshops and sell advance copies
ready for the publication date. All this meant his work took up much more
time than usual, and Shepard, now represented by the leading literary
agent Spencer Curtis Brown, agreed a fairer remuneration with Milne, who
genuinely recognised Shepard's contribution. This change was intended
both to acknowledge the key part played by Shepard in the creation of the
books, and also to ensure a more equitable financial arrangement.

Shepard always worked hard on his research and continued to spend
much time in and around the Ashdown Forest, paying particular attention
to the stands of trees and the general vegetation. Indeed, it is often remarked
that on occasion it looks as though he created careful and representative
landscapes into which he inserted sometimes cartoon-like characters.

Preliminary sketches for Chapter 9,
and the final illustration.

These two small drawings also relate to Chapter 9, when Piglet is marooned in his house by water. We see a rather charming domestic scene of Piglet standing on a stool in his kitchen, looking out of the window as the wind blows in (*above*), and Piglet throwing his bottle out of the window to call for help (*left*).

An early pencil sketch of Winnie-the-Pooh
using Christopher Robin's umbrella as a boat.

Winnie-the-Pooh was obviously all about Pooh, and Shepard drew heavily
on Growler for inspiration (who remained at home at Shamley Green as
a model) to create the marvellous images of a larger-than-life character,
stuffed full of human traits and foibles. One original drawing which Shepard
kept for himself was the picture of Winnie-the-Pooh standing on tiptoes
on a chair to reach a jar of honey. The other characters were introduced
chapter by chapter, so that we meet Winnie-the-Pooh in Chapter 1, Rabbit
in Chapter 2, Piglet in Chapter 3, Eeyore in Chapter 4, and so on. Shepard
used toys from Christopher Robin's nursery, many bought from Harrods
and some, later, purchased specifically for the purpose, to create Piglet,
Eeyore, Kanga and Roo. Owl and Rabbit (and all Rabbit's 'friends and
relations') were from Milne's imagination and not based on any real-life
toys, and so Shepard had to use his own creative talents to bring these
characters to life. Shepard continued to use his sketches of Graham as a
young boy as the basis for the drawings of Christopher Robin, sometimes
marrying these with images of the real Christopher Robin. He drew sketch
after preparatory sketch, working to get exactly the right image to illustrate

the correct part of the story, and in response to Milne's and Methuen's reactions.

Winnie-the-Pooh was published in London on 14 October 1926 – and in New York on 21 October – to even greater acclaim. In the UK, Methuen's first print run totalled 32,000 this time, and entirely justified Lucas's optimism, while in America 150,000 copies had been sold by the end of the year. The book was immediately reprinted and, of course, has never been out of print. Clearly on the crest of a wave of critical and commercial success, Lucas once more urged Milne and Shepard forward towards book number three.

Shepard and Milne had torn up the rulebook and made the public look at literature, and particularly children's literature, in a different way. Rather than reading *to* children, the books inspired authors and illustrators

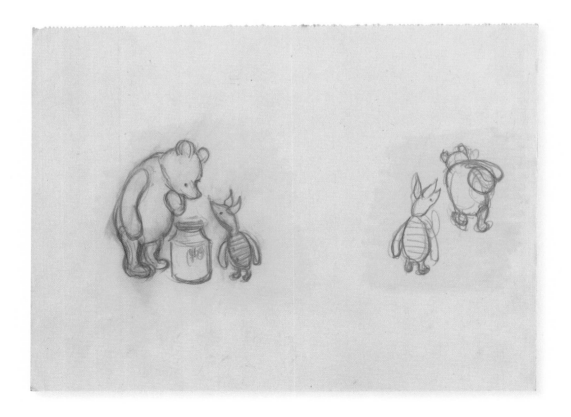

These two pencil drawings were probably early suggestions for Chapter 6.

Published illustrations showing some of Milnes's principal characters.

An early pencil version of Piglet running towards Christopher Robin crying out 'Help a horrible Heffalump'.

to write *for* children, and in the period up to the Second World War, this opportunity for adults and children to sit and enjoy books together grew rapidly. *The Story of Babar* was first published in 1931, and *Orlando the Marmalade Cat* in 1938, both following this model of stories that integrated words and pictures in a seamless format.

"Took down a very large jar of Honey"

Shepard kept this illustration, 'Took down a very large jar of Honey', in his own personal archive.

CHAPTER 5

Now We Are Six

The second volume of poems was published on 13 October 1927 in both Britain and America, and was a follow-on from *When We Were Very Young*. Indeed, Milne himself wrote, 'We have been nearly three years writing this book. We began it when we were very young ... and now we are six.'

The poems had been written spasmodically from 1924 onwards, and over half had already been written when *Winnie-the-Pooh* was published. Some had been published in various periodicals, and some were already illustrated by Shepard, although when brought together for book publication a number of changes were made. For instance, Shepard wrote in his own hand on a copy of the poem originally called 'Dinkie' that the title had later been changed to 'Binker'.

The book was dedicated 'To *Anne Darlington* now she is seven and because she is so speshal', and Milne implied that the book had been 'promised' to Anne, who was the daughter of W. A. Darlington, both a personal friend of Milne and an influential theatre critic for the *Daily Telegraph*. His youngest daughter, Anne was Christopher Robin's closest friend; they went to the same school in Chelsea, and later Anne often came to stay at Cotchford Farm, sometimes without her parents. In Shepard's private papers there are a number of photographs of Christopher Robin and Anne, which may have been taken by Shepard himself on one of his periodic visits to Cotchford

*Christopher Robin Milne
+ Ann
in their Sussex Garden*

Christopher Robin Milne and Anne Darlington at Cotchford Farm, with Shepard's description on the reverse.

A page from Shepard's sketchbook showing a tree with careful notes for when the sketch was later worked up – possibly as a model for 'The Charcoal-Burner'.

Very rough early
drafts for 'Us Two'
(*above*), and one of the
published illustrations
(*opposite*).

Farm. Shepard seems to have used these photographs for the drawings for
two particular poems in the collection: 'Buttercup Days', which refers to both
Anne and Christopher Robin by name, and shows them together, heads bent
over the buttercups and with Cotchford Farm clearly in the background (see
page 77), and later in 'The Good Little Girl'.

Shepard continued to research meticulously and to sketch many
preliminary drawings; the carefully annotated pencil sketch of a tree (see
previous page), which may have been for the country scene of 'The Charcoal-
Burner', shows the detail he put into what are, at first glance, simple and

uncomplicated images. There is a wonderful set of two draft pencil drawings for 'The Little Black Hen' that show great character and movement in the figures, with a totally convincing farmyard setting, undoubtedly drawn from life (see overleaf).

There are also a considerable number of pencil sketches in Shepard's sketchbooks from this time that don't appear to have been used for this collection. Shepard would draw images almost always from life and then decide where to use them; sometimes this would be much later, as with the drawings of his son, Graham, made in the years before the First World War

First sketch p. 60

Two preliminary pencil sketches for 'The Little Black Hen'
(*above*). Unusually, both were fully signed by Shepard. The final
published illustrations appear below.

First sketch for "The little black hen"
N.W.A.S.   p. 61

Pencil sketch of a girl, probably from the mid-1920s. Shepard kept hold of these sketches and sometimes used them as inspiration in later work.

but not used until decades later as models for Christopher Robin.

By now, author and illustrator understood well each other's ways of working, although not everything was predictable and there would still be the occasional surprise, as when, for example, an illustration planned for a right-hand page suddenly had to become a left-hand one. Each change such as this required Shepard to go back and edit his illustration to make it 'work'. His 'free hand' was still being exercised, and it's interesting to note that Shepard introduced more of Christopher Robin's toys into his illustrations, even when these were not mentioned by Milne in the text.

One of the most interesting drawings is the only illustration for 'Waiting at the Window', which shows Pooh, Eeyore and Piglet – these seem to have been Christopher Robin's favourites – at the window of a London house, but with a noticeably different Christopher Robin, who seems older, more of a schoolboy than a young child, with shorter, more tousled hair. This may well be because the real Christopher Robin was getting older, and the illustrations simply reflected this. The original proposed endpiece for the book, showing Christopher Robin, Pooh and Piglet sitting together in the hollow of an old tree, was not used because the drawings of Christopher Robin looked

The published illustration for 'Waiting at the Window'
showing a more mature Christopher Robin.

Sketch for The End (not used)

This sketch of Christopher Robin, Pooh and Piglet in the
hollow of a tree (*above*) was proposed as the closing illustration
for *Now We Are Six* but was replaced by the well-known image
of them jumping in the air (*opposite*).

unconvincing – the pose looked uncomfortable and ill at ease – so this was
replaced by the very recognisable and iconic drawing of Christopher Robin,
Pooh and Piglet all jumping in the air.

Finally, the collection was ready. However, about two weeks before
publication in October 1927, an unexpected tragedy engulfed the Shepard
family. Shepard's wife, Pie, had been suffering increasingly from asthma,

'The End'

and they had been advised to move from Shamley Green to higher ground, where the air would be clearer. Consequently, they bought a plot of land on a well-elevated site at Pewley Down, on the south side of Guildford, and commissioned a handsome house, the family finances being now on a much more stable footing. The house was well advanced when it was decided that Pie needed a routine nasal operation to relieve some of the symptoms of her asthma. She entered a London nursing home for this relatively minor procedure, but inexplicably died under the anaesthetic. This was a shattering and totally unexpected blow for Shepard and his children. Graham, now twenty, was an undergraduate at Lincoln College, Oxford, and Mary,

Sketch work for 'The Friend'.

Ernest Shepard at his new house, Long Meadow
in Guildford, in the late 1920s.

Colour draft for a dust jacket, from the 1950s or 1960s.

seventeen, was living at home and preparing to go to art school. Pie had been the love of Shepard's life, his soulmate, his rock, and possibly in part a maternal figure, taking the place of his greatly beloved mother. He was left stunned, and for the first time in his adult life he did not use his sketchbook daily.

A fortnight later, *Now We Are Six* was published to yet further critical acclaim and high sales, with 90,000 copies pre-ordered in America alone. Methuen apparently viewed its popularity over *When We Were Very Young* as being in part due to the more frequent appearances of Winnie-the-Pooh. Understandably, Shepard was unable to join in the general rejoicing and enthusiasm that greeted another successful volume from the Milne and Shepard partnership. Gradually, keeping his personal feelings to himself, and while supporting Graham and Mary as best he could, Shepard returned to, and became immersed in, his work.

The new house in Guildford was completed in due course, and the Shepards moved into their new home in 1928. Although at first Shepard found it difficult to adjust to his changed surroundings (he now had a splendid new studio within the house, rather than an outbuilding in the garden) he soon came around to the new set-up, and started to create new and exciting images for Milne's next outing for Winnie-the-Pooh in the final book, which would become *The House at Pooh Corner*.

CHAPTER 6

The House at Pooh Corner

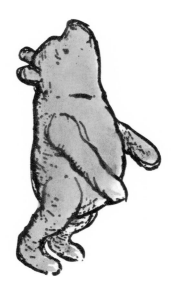

In October 1928, barely a year after the publication of *Now We Are Six*, came *The House at Pooh Corner*, a triumphant finale to the four books, which contained a further ten chapters of stories. Milne made it quite clear from the 'Contradiction' – instead of an Introduction – at the start of the book, that this was going to be the final outing for Winnie-the-Pooh, saying '… Christopher Robin and his friends, who have already been introduced to you, are now going to say Good-bye.' In the view of many commentators over the years, *The House at Pooh Corner* is a better book than *Winnie-the-Pooh*, with

Early draft for the penultimate illustration in Chapter 1
showing Christopher Robin, Piglet and Winnie-the-Pooh
in the snow.

stronger storylines, the introduction of Tigger and more engaging adventures – allowing Milne and Shepard to end their collaboration on a high. And so, in this final volume, we find two of the most resonant images ever drawn by Shepard: Tigger and Poohsticks.

By this time, the Milne–Shepard collaboration was a well-oiled machine. They now met less frequently, as they simply had no need to do so; they knew instinctively what was necessary, and seem often to have anticipated the other's particular requirements. In this book, carrying on from the illustration in 'Waiting at the Window' from the previous book, we see an even older Christopher Robin, with longer legs and a greater difference in size between him and the animals. Again, Shepard used drawings of his son, Graham, at the age of seven to eight, as a model. In fact, Shepard was already working on the illustrations for *The House at Pooh Corner* while he was finishing the illustrations for *Now We Are Six*.

"Saw Piglet setting in his best arm chair"

Early pencil sketch of Winnie-the-Pooh and Piglet.

Unused pencil drawing of Winnie-the-Pooh and
Piglet in hats, coats, scarves and boots in the snow.

The stories start in the winter, with the first chapter centring on the
principal characters making a home for Eeyore. All of the illustrations after the
first one are in the snow, and Shepard made numerous preparatory sketches for
these, many of which were not used in the final edition. There is a wonderful
early sketch of Winnie-the-Pooh and Piglet dressed up for the snow, in hats,
coats and boots (above), although this seems to have been discarded as an
option at a fairly early stage. It is interesting how the addition of hats changes

Unused sketch showing Pooh and Piglet singing Pooh's
'Outdoor Song which Has To Be Sung In The Snow'.

the impression of both characters – they both seem more constrained, less free
and perhaps more human when wrapped up for the cold.

In the next chapter we are introduced to Tigger, an inspirational addition
to the characters of the Hundred Acre Wood, with Shepard somehow conjuring
up the impression of a tiger cub crossed with a Labrador puppy. Even Milne
was excited, writing to Shepard, 'I'm longing to see the "Tigger" illustrations!'
Tigger is bouncy, energetic and enthusiastic, and Shepard manages to convey

An early sketch (*above*) and the final, published illustration (*below*), introducing one of the most recognisable characters in the Hundred Acre Wood: Tigger.

the whole sense of his movement with just a few lines, often drawing Tigger slightly higher than the surroundings, as if he has just bounced in. The strokes and block colouring of the stripes are simple yet hugely effective; the rounded nose, forward-facing whiskers and huge eyes with a perpetual air of surprise make Shepard's interpretation the very embodiment of the Tigger we know and love.

Shepard's early attempt at illustrating Tigger's introduction to the other creatures in the wood, as they try to help find out what Tiggers eat, at first involved Piglet. However, as Pooh's enormous relief that Tigger did not like honey became the focus, Piglet was dropped. We have a very interesting early drawing (below) which shows how Shepard worked – he draws Pooh's right arm in at least three potential positions to determine which would look more natural, and also fit best with the narrative of the story.

We next move to the Heffalump trap, where Pooh and Piglet end up in the bottom of the trap. Shepard's original illustration for this sequence shows them sitting at the bottom of the 'Heffalump Trap for Poohs!', the 'Bear of

Early sketch showing Winnie-the-Pooh and Piglet trying to find out what Tiggers like to eat. In the final version Piglet was omitted.

P 4³   "He'll say HO-HO"

4.P.C.

An early alternative (*above*) and final version (*below*) of Winnie-the-Pooh and Piglet having fallen into Piglet's Heffalump trap.

Very Little Brain' with his left paw up to his mouth, seemingly confused, and Piglet looking anxiously towards him for inspiration (opposite). In the end, this was replaced by the image of Pooh having actually landed right on top of Piglet, looking bewildered at not being able to work out where he can hear Piglet's voice coming from. Shepard seems to have greatly enjoyed drawing Piglet, for there are many sketches and preliminary drawings of him – in fact, almost as many as for Winnie-the-Pooh. Piglet was closely modelled on Christopher Robin's own toy named Piglet, and usually shown in his stripy costume (and later, when in colour, in green). Unusually, Shepard kept a sequence of finished Piglet drawings from the *The House at Pooh Corner* for himself, and one feels he had a special affection in his heart for the plucky little piglet; these drawings (see overleaf) show him 'planting a haycorn, Pooh, so it can grow up into an oak-tree, and have lots of haycorns just outside the front door instead of having to walk miles and miles, do you see, Pooh?' As with a number of the original illustrations, these were exhibited for sale in the late 1920s at The Sporting Gallery, a fashionable commercial art gallery in London's Mayfair, and are marked at four guineas each, later reduced to three guineas – but presumably these were unsold or withdrawn by Shepard.

And so to the perennially popular Poohsticks! Shepard took this simple concept from Milne's narrative and through his timeless images set in train an enduring pastime across the globe; just think how many millions of children (and adults) have played Poohsticks over the ensuing century.

Shepard took some liberties with the bridge in the Ashdown Forest where Christopher Robin and Pooh played Poohsticks. The original was a wooden structure, not particularly robust but with a rustic charm. Shepard's first black-and-white version was drawn with brick piers and wooden balustrades above, shown on page 104 with Eeyore having floated upside-down under the bridge; although his later full-page colour drawing shows a brick arch with what look rather like ranch-style white railings. But how did Eeyore fall into the river? Of course, he was 'bounced', and an initial unpublished pencil sketch shows Eeyore and Tigger, in bouncy mode, by the edge of the riverbank. The last picture in this story, that of Christopher Robin leaning over the bridge, with Pooh and Piglet beside him, must be one of the most recognisable children's illustrations of all time.

Shepard kept this original sequence of drawings of Piglet for himself. The image on the bottom right (*opposite*) shows the reverse marked for a potential sale at 3 (4 crossed out) guineas. Presumably it either did not sell or Shepard withdrew it from sale.

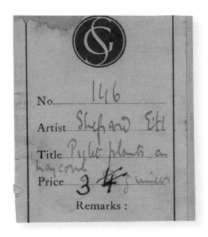

A very early draft of
Eeyore upside-down,
having floated under
the Poohsticks bridge.

P. 79

Reduce to 5 3/4"

Eeyore and Tigger on the riverbank. Possibly an early option
for the scene where Eeyore is 'bounced' into the river and
swept under the Poohsticks bridge.

The image we all remember: Winnie-the-Pooh, Piglet
and Christopher Robin playing Poohsticks.

Minette Shepard, granddaughter of E. H.
Shepard, and bear.

Another star of *The House at Pooh Corner* was, of course, Eeyore. Shepard had a great fondness for Eeyore, and gradually developed the character from his first appearances in *Winnie-the-Pooh*, enhancing his wonderfully gloomy approach to life and providing a counter balance to Tigger's bouncy optimism and zest for life. Shepard's imagery was so clever that the picture of Eeyore floating in the water, drawn simply as four upturned paws and a splash, is instantly and unmistakeably Eeyore.

At the end of the book, Milne reiterates that this is the final chapter: the stories have come to an end, and it is time to move on. Shepard illustrates this poignantly, drawing just Christopher Robin and Pooh as they walk up towards Galleons Lap and the highest point of the Enchanted Places and so to the end of the adventure – finally concluding with a silhouette of Pooh and Christopher Robin skipping into the future.

And so what of Growler, the model for Winnie-the-Pooh, who in due course was passed on to Graham Shepard's daughter, Minette, and indeed, of Piglet? Let Shepard end by telling this story in his own words.

Handwritten paragraph in which Shepard explains what happened to his models for Winnie-the-Pooh and Piglet.

CHAPTER 7

Expanding
the Image

While A. A. Milne wrote no more about Winnie-the-Pooh, Christopher Robin and the animals of the Hundred Acre Wood after the publication of *The House at Pooh Corner*, instead turning with relief to other projects, Shepard's magic continued to be in great demand. As the popularity of the four original books continued to soar, Methuen in the UK, Dutton in the USA and a range of other publishers in overseas territories brought out new editions and versions of the books, and many of these needed adapted illustrations, as page sizes and layout changed.

In addition, the images of Winnie-the-Pooh and friends proved ideal for merchandising. This was an area in which the United States already led, and in 1931 Milne licensed the Pooh 'franchise' in North America to Stephen Slesinger, the American film, TV and radio producer who became known as the father of the licensing industry. Slesinger was astute and innovative, promoting and enhancing the 'Pooh' image for the next thirty years, and much of what he developed successfully in America travelled back over the pond to the UK and even further afield. Merchandise ranged from soft toys based on the original animals, to clothing, household goods and much more. In London, Methuen also recognised the books' potential, and embarked on an expansion of what would later be called a 'brand'.

The first music book to be published was *Fourteen Songs*, published by Dutton in New York in 1925, which incorporated verses from *When We Were Very Young* with a piano score, and which was decorated with Shepard's illustrations. The British edition had been dedicated to Her Royal Highness Princess Mary, the only daughter of King George V, and her two sons. In the next music book, the dedication was inscribed to Her Royal Highness Princess Elizabeth, then elder daughter of Their Royal Highnesses the Duke and Duchess of York, (and now, of course, Her Majesty The Queen). This connection to royalty was managed by E. V. Lucas who well understood, and wished to make use of, the immense popularity of the royal family in the 1920s, and these dedications added a certain extra sparkle and lustre to the Pooh phenomenon.

A rare presentation copy of the first edition of *The Hums of Pooh* signed by A. A. Milne, H. Fraser-Simson and E. H. Shepard.

THE HUMS OF POOH

LYRICS BY

POOH

MUSIC BY

H. FRASER-SIMSON

INTRODUCTION AND NOTES BY

A. A. MILNE

DECORATIONS BY

E. H. SHEPARD

ADDITIONAL LYRIC BY

EEYORE

THE WHOLE PRESENTED TO THE PUBLIC

BY

METHUEN & CO., LTD.

36, ESSEX STREET, LONDON, W.C.

IN CONJUNCTION WITH

ASCHERBERG, HOPWOOD & CREW, LTD.

16, MORTIMER STREET, LONDON, W.

Isn't it Funny . . . .

One day when Pooh was out walking, he came to a very tall tree, and from the top of the tree there came a loud buzzing noise. Well, Pooh knew what that meant—honey ; so he began to climb the tree. And as he climbed, he sang a little song to himself. Really it was two little songs, because he climbed twenty-seven feet nine-and-a-half inches in between the two verses. So if the second verse is higher than the first, you will know why.

The text sat opposite the opening bars of each song, with an additional explanation where necessary, as shown here.

The music for these songs had been composed by Harold Fraser-Simson, a well-known composer of light music, who was a neighbour and acquaintance of Milne; and in 1929 Methuen commissioned a further music book, *The Hums of Pooh*. The presentation copy shown here was made specially for Shepard and is one of very few remaining books that are personally signed by both A. A. Milne and E. H. Shepard. The first song, predictably, began with 'Isn't it funny how a bear likes honey', and each song was given its own introduction. Throughout the book, Shepard's original illustrations are re-used and adapted, although he had to tweak them to work more closely with the new format; for example, on the first page of music where the tree from Chapter 1 of *Winnie-the-Pooh* is reproduced, you can see that Shepard has added to the swarm of bees moving from the trees towards the title of the song. In an age when most middle-class homes had a piano and when the wireless, in its infancy, did not offer much entertainment for children, these music books were hugely popular, encouraging parents and children to gather round the piano and sing together.

First bars of 'Isn't it Funny' showing how the original
drawings were rescaled to fit the larger page size.

Front cover of the 'Pooh Calendar' for 1930, showing
Shepard's illustrations of the principal characters from
the Hundred Acre Wood.

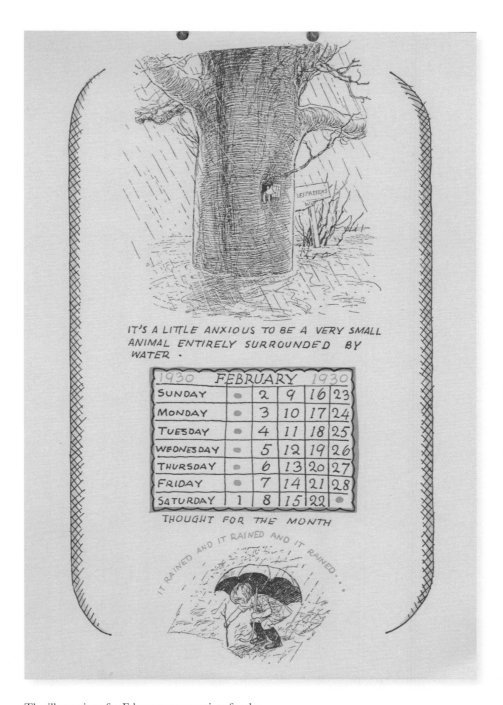

The illustrations for February, appropriate for the
month, are from Chapter 9 of *Winnie-the-Pooh*.

And so the bandwagon had started to roll. The four original books had all been published in black and white, but colour was becoming more accessible and affordable for publishers. Gradually, demand grew for colour – first for coloured dust jackets, and later with spot colour on a limited number of pages. It was apparently Stephen Slesinger who gave Winnie-the-Pooh his red top in the 1930s. Interestingly, and shortly after Milne unexpectedly had a stroke in the early 1950s, Slesinger commissioned Pooh illustrations from another artist. The experiment was not a success, and was never repeated; strangely, no record seems to exist of these alternative drawings, which sank without trace.

The merchandise opportunities kept coming, such as the 1930 Pooh Calendar that Shepard created for Methuen, designing a new front cover but recycling the original illustrations from *Winnie-the-Pooh*. Another project came in the form of a moveable model of Christopher Robin, which Shepard drew with all its moving parts.

Shepard found himself increasingly busy as the 1930s progressed. Not only was he fulfilling additional work on Winnie-the-Pooh projects, but he was also working for *Punch* on a weekly basis and undertaking a wide range of commissions, many for book illustrations. Milne had not finished with Shepard either. He had been hugely impressed and influenced by Kenneth Grahame's *The Wind in the Willows*, first published in 1908, and which many felt had influenced his approach to writing for children. Milne had persuaded Grahame to allow him to dramatise the book into a stage play – eventually becoming *Toad of Toad Hall* – and he had been working on it, on and off (with Fraser-Simson composing the music), throughout the 1920s. During this time, Milne became increasingly aware of how dissatisfied Grahame was with the various attempts to illustrate *The Wind in the Willows* and he persuaded Shepard, who had already illustrated Grahame's *The Golden Age* and *Dream Days*, to approach Grahame – but this time with Milne's personal recommendation – to make a fresh attempt at capturing the essence of the animals of the riverbank and the wild wood. Initially, Shepard was cautious and Grahame was anxious, but the resulting illustrations were a triumph, both with Kenneth Grahame and the public, and have never since been out of print.

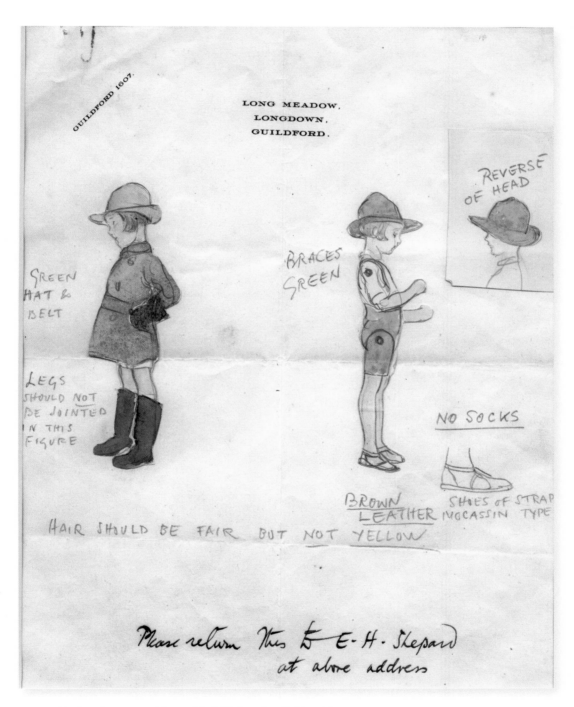

Designs for a moveable model of Christopher Robin with
instructions, drawn on Shepard's home writing paper.

Familiar illustrations from *The Wind in the Willows*, drawn by Shepard.

As Shepard's reputation soared, he was obliged, due to pressure of work, to decline certain commissions, including one to illustrate *Mary Poppins* by P. L. Travers. By a complete coincidence the commission was then awarded to Shepard's daughter, Mary, a distinguished illustrator in her own right, who went on to illustrate all of the Mary Poppins books from 1934 to 1988.

Both Milne and Shepard maintained long working relationships with *Punch*, extending for many years after the publication of the Pooh books. In 1932 Owen Seaman retired, and E. V. Knox was appointed Editor – known as Evoe, he was already a close friend of Shepard. In 1937 Evoe, also

Mary Shepard, E. H. Shepard's daughter, illustrated all the Mary Poppins books after her father turned down the commission. This volume was inscribed by P. L. Travers to Mary Shepard's great-niece, Arabella.

a widower, married Shepard's daughter, Mary. Despite the age gap – Evoe was a contemporary of Shepard's – it was a happy and enduring marriage, and Mary became very close to her stepchildren, Rawle Knox, the distinguished foreign correspondent, and Penelope Fitzgerald, the Booker Prize-winning author.

As Shepard took up the critical role of principal cartoonist for *Punch* in the mid-1930s, now responsible for the lead political cartoon each week, he became even busier. In this role, he contributed to the editorial stance of the magazine over a significant period that covered the rise of the Nazis in Germany, the abdication crisis of 1936, the appeasement movement and the Munich Agreement of 1938, the descent into war and the appointment of Winston Churchill as wartime prime minister. Commuting from Guildford became too time-consuming, so during the week he lived in a house in Melina Place, in St John's Wood and close to Evoe and Mary, later sharing the house with his son, Graham, also an artist, illustrator and writer, and Graham's wife, Ann. Later still, the household would be extended with the addition of Graham and Ann's baby daughter, Minette, to whom Shepard was to become extremely close. Shepard returned to Long Meadow at weekends, when his children and their friends were often there.

At the outbreak of the Second World War in 1939, Shepard immediately volunteered for the local Home Guard in Guildford, and, in addition to his professional commitments, was out on duty, often at night – and by this time at the age of sixty. Melina Place was badly damaged by enemy action during the Blitz, and Shepard had to relocate his London studio. However, a much worse blow fell in 1943 when Graham, who had volunteered for the Royal Naval Volunteer Reserve, was killed in the North Atlantic when his ship HMS *Polyanthus* was torpedoed and sank. Shepard's daughter-in-law, Ann, and granddaughter, Minette, were in Canada with Ann's family, and Shepard became increasingly lonely.

Earlier in the war he had met Norah Carroll, a nurse from St Mary's Hospital in Paddington, at a concert in London. They started to see each other regularly, and shortly after Graham's death they became engaged and were married later in 1943. They divided their time between London and Long Meadow, and Norah provided Shepard with a sense of stability and an ordered home life, something which had been missing, certainly during the early part of the war.

Milne continued to submit pieces for *Punch* through the 1930s and 1940s, but increasingly his light and frivolous style, which had so caught the public mood in the 1920s, failed to resonate as the reading public's taste moved on. Having had at one time four plays simultaneously running in the West End of London in the 1920s, Milne had none of his plays staged after the late 1930s; and although he continued to submit work to *Punch*, by the 1940s E. V. Knox had to write to Milne to explain that while his writing was as good as it had ever been, the public was no longer receptive to his whimsical style and, with regret, *Punch* would no longer be able to publish Milne's contributions in the future. It was a difficult and sad end to a forty-year relationship.

Shepard and his second wife, Norah, after the Second World War.

CHAPTER 8

The Twilight Years

After the end of the Second World War, Shepard was as busy as ever. He continued as principal cartoonist for *Punch* for a further ten years, documenting the political upheavals of the 1940s Labour government, many of which would define the post-war era in Britain – including the creation of the National Health Service and the widespread nationalisation of key public services. He continued to draw illustrations for books and designed dust jackets, and worked on a range of projects and activities that would have exhausted a man half his age (in

Study for cover design
E H Shepard

A post Second World War, full-page, colour illustration of
Winnie-the-Pooh and the characters from the Hundred
Acre Wood (*opposite*) and the original study (*above*).

1945 he was sixty-five) and, of course, he had a constant stream of ongoing work for Winnie-the-Pooh. Much of this was to do with both the continued expansion of the 'brand', with spin-off after spin-off, but also due to the increasingly widespread introduction of colour into printing processes. Shepard and Norah now lived full-time at Long Meadow, and he had the great joy of having his granddaughter, Minette (who had returned from Canada with her mother at the end of the war), growing up close by in Puttenham. Neither Shepard's brother nor sister had had any children, and his daughter Mary, too, had remained childless, so Minette was his only grandchild, and he saw a good deal of her as she grew up.

A. A. Milne died in 1956, at the age of seventy-four, having been an invalid since suffering a stroke several years earlier. Although the two were never personal friends, Milne and Shepard had kept in touch over the years, not least due to joint business issues connected to the Pooh stories, and Shepard was saddened by the end of a long-standing professional collaboration that had achieved so much for so many. In Milne's obituaries he was much praised for the Winnie-the-Pooh books, although personally he would probably have been disappointed not to have been principally remembered for his adult poetry and plays.

While Shepard was to outlive Milne for a good few decades, the mid-1950s saw Shepard taking a step back from his busy career. In 1953, Malcolm Muggeridge became Editor of *Punch*, and almost immediately dispensed with Shepard's services as principal cartoonist with apparently little recognition of his significant commitment to the magazine. While probably ready for retirement – he had been in this position for seventeen years and was seventy-three years old – Shepard was nonetheless saddened by the manner of his departure from *Punch*, having been published there for nearly fifty years.

No longer needing to commute to London each week, and with Minette now grown up and pursuing her own life in London, the Shepards decided that Long Meadow was too big for them, and they moved to the village of Lodsworth in rural Sussex, where Shepard spent the remainder of his long life. Freedom from the weekly timetable of *Punch* also enabled him to turn to a project he had long been considering: writing his autobiography, which he started in earnest in 1956. The first book, *Drawn from Memory*, was published in 1957, a charming description of a year in his Victorian childhood, and was extremely well received both by critics and the public.

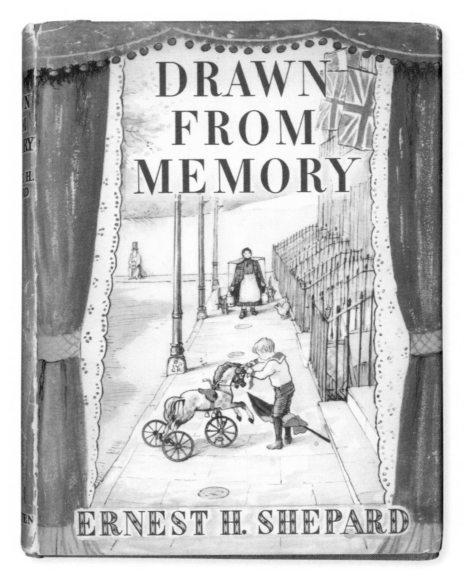

Dust jacket for Shepard's first book of memoirs, *Drawn from Memory*, featuring Shepard's own illustration.

An early sketch for the cover
of Dutton's *The Pooh Song Book*.

Work for Winnie-the-Pooh also continued apace. The American market in particular appeared to enjoy an insatiable appetite for new and reworked illustrations. Christopher Robin's original toys were now in the USA permanently; Dutton and Slesinger had asked for their loan for publicity purposes in 1947, and they had profitably toured North America ever since. For no obvious reason, the Milnes did not ask for their return, although the toys did pay two visits back to their homeland: once was in 1969 to complement an exhibition of Pooh illustrations to mark Shepard's ninetieth birthday. In 1987 Dutton presented them to the New York Public Library, where they remain today. Occasionally, visitors are disappointed to see that the 'real' Winnie-the-Pooh – Christopher Robin's teddy bear – does not resemble the bear in the stories, but, as we know, sadly Growler was not able to take his rightful place in this assembly.

In the late 1950s Dutton decided to amalgamate the musical publications, including the original Fraser-Simson book *The Hums of Pooh*, into one volume called *The Pooh Song Book*. All the main characters are there in musical mode, with Pooh conducting, accompanied by Piglet on the grand piano, and the others struggling, to a greater or lesser extent,

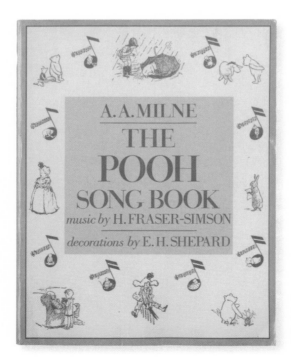

The cover of a Dutton edition dating from the 1980s.

with sheet music (Tigger looks as though he is about to eat his). Shepard produced many designs along these lines for new editions and versions of the stories, but perhaps one of his most challenging commissions was to illustrate *Winnie Ille Pu*, the Latin edition.

The great success of *Drawn from Memory*, which seemed to have touched a chord with its description of a single year in Shepard's childhood, led to a further volume, *Drawn from Life*, published in 1961. This took Shepard's personal story from his schooldays up until his marriage to Pie, and the very positive reaction to this second volume encouraged Shepard to write and illustrate two books of children's stories himself: *Ben & Brock* in 1965 and *Betsy & Joe* in 1966. The style of the illustrations in these two books is more loosely connected to *The Wind in the Willows* than Winnie-the-Pooh. In that same year, 1966, the one millionth copy of the original *Winnie-the-Pooh* book was sold by a bookshop in Bristol.

Meanwhile, demand from abroad for Winnie-the-Pooh, particularly from America, continued to soar. Slesinger and Daphne Milne agreed terms with Disney in 1961 for the animation rights to be exploited, and since then Disney has taken an increasing role in promoting and expanding the Pooh franchise. Later on the original Disney cartoons from the 1960s were widely derided by the purists as being simplistic and having none of the Shepard

Illustrations from *Ben & Brock*, one of the children's books authored and illustrated by Shepard.

An incongruous sight: Winnie Ille Pu, drawn by Shepard as a Roman bust complete with laurel wreath for the Latin translation by Alexander Lenard.

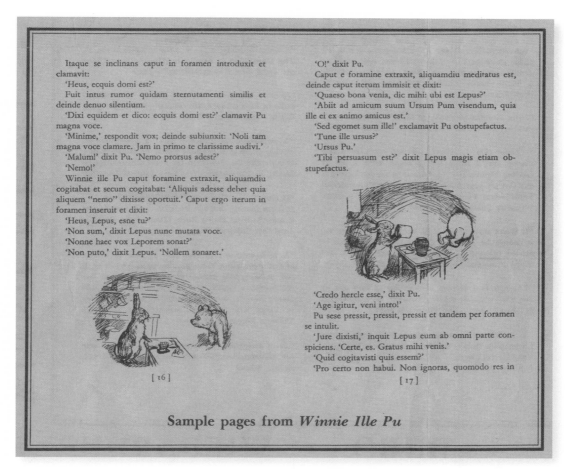

Itaque se inclinans caput in foramen introduxit et clamavit:

'Heus, ecquis domi est?'

Fuit intus rumor quidam sternutamenti similis et deinde denuo silentium.

'Dixi equidem et dico: ecquis domi est?' clamavit Pu magna voce.

'Minime,' respondit vox; deinde subiunxit: 'Noli tam magna voce clamare. Jam in primo te clarissime audivi.'

'Malum!' dixit Pu. 'Nemo prorsus adest?'

'Nemo!'

Winnie ille Pu caput foramine extraxit, aliquamdiu cogitabat et secum cogitabat: 'Aliquis adesse debet quia aliquem "nemo" dixisse oportuit.' Caput ergo iterum in foramen inseruit et dixit:

'Heus, Lepus, esne tu?'

'Non sum,' dixit Lepus nunc mutata voce.

'Nonne haec vox Leporem sonat?'

'Non puto,' dixit Lepus. 'Nollem sonaret.'

[16]

'O!' dixit Pu.

Caput e foramine extraxit, aliquamdiu meditatus est, deinde caput iterum immisit et dixit:

'Quaeso bona venia, dic mihi: ubi est Lepus?'

'Abiit ad amicum suum Ursum Pum visendum, quia ille ei ex animo amicus est.'

'Sed egomet sum ille!' exclamavit Pu obstupefactus.

'Tune ille ursus?'

'Ursus Pu.'

'Tibi persuasum est?' dixit Lepus magis etiam obstupefactus.

'Credo hercle esse,' dixit Pu.

'Age igitur, veni intro!'

Pu sese pressit, pressit, pressit et tandem per foramen se intulit.

'Jure dixisti,' inquit Lepus eum ab omni parte conspiciens. 'Certe, es. Gratus mihi venis.'

'Quid cogitavisti quis essem?'

'Pro certo non habui. Non ignoras, quomodo res in

[17]

Sample pages from *Winnie Ille Pu*

A sample page with the original drawings of Pooh and Rabbit.

Disney reinvented Pooh and his friends
for the big screen.

Draft for a title page – probably early 1960s.

Shepard's version of the Bayeux Tapestry depicting the characters of
the Hundred Acre Wood and the colours of the Tricolore. The design
was intended for the cover of a French edition of *Winnie-the-Pooh*.

magic, but over the years Disney's approach became more sophisticated and nuanced and increasingly aligned with the Shepard originals. The President of the United States of America Lyndon Johnson's daughter Lynda was a great fan of Winnie-the-Pooh, and even invited the Shepards to her White House wedding, which they were sadly unable to attend (incidentally, one of the wedding gifts was a specially commissioned set of Winnie-the-Pooh china). However, the First Lady, Lady Bird Johnson, later made a personal visit to Shepard in Lodsworth for tea, demonstrating her affection for Pooh Bear.

Parts of a "Pooh" orchestra

Ernest H Shepard
November 1970

Piglet attempts three instruments with verve and brio, while
Eeyore, in characteristically gloomy mood, tussles with the tuba.

Shepard in his studio with his watercolours in the 1960s.

And still the demands from publishers and agents flowed in – a dust jacket for a French edition of the original Winnie-the-Pooh book from this time is particularly memorable (see page 134). Shepard, by his own account, enjoyed these colour exercises, which was just as well as he was often asked to produce multiple options for new titles, and then to re-execute them for different markets. *The Pooh Cook Book* was a great success, and was printed in a number of countries. In the British version, the recipes were written by the then doyenne of cookery writers, Katie Stewart of *The Times*.

> Embridge Forge
> Dartmouth
> Devon
> 16 12 74
>
> Dear Mr Shepard.
>
> This is to remind you of how and where it all started, and – I hope – to revive some happy memories of Cotchford Farm and of my parents.
>
> Methuen wanted to include some of your drawings alongside some of my photographs to show
>
> how closely fiction followed fact. I left the selection of both to them, and I imagine they asked you about it first. I have said a public thank you in the book. But I would like to add a private thank you in this letter.
>
> With all good wishes
> Yours sincerely
> Christopher Milne

Christopher Robin Milne's handwritten letter to Shepard sent shortly after Shepard's ninety-fifth birthday.

Towards the end of his long life, Shepard became interested in the legacy of Winnie-the-Pooh and, following a successful exhibition of the original drawings at the Victoria and Albert Museum in London in 1969, he donated over 300 illustrations to the museum's permanent collection. In 1972, he made a further substantial donation of personal papers, artefacts, drawings, illustrations and correspondence to the University of Surrey, in recognition of his close connection with the county in which he had lived for over fifty years. In the same year, and perhaps a little overdue, Shepard was awarded an OBE in the Queen's Birthday Honours. It joined his Military Cross from 1917, for conspicuous gallantry during the First World War, which had been personally awarded by The Queen's grandfather King George V, some fifty-five years before.

Christopher Robin Milne maintained a friendly relationship with Shepard, exchanging occasional letters and Christmas cards, and in 1974 sent him a copy of his reminiscences, *The Enchanted Places*, with the inscription, 'For Ernest Shepard, who added so much of his own very special magic to that of the Enchanted Places'. He also sent a charming letter with a private 'thank you' for everything Shepard had done (see previous page).

Towards the end of his life, Shepard lived quietly in Lodsworth, and was often seen walking around the village, although with increasingly poor eyesight. He and Norah travelled less, due to his increasing infirmity, but he continued to draw regularly, and was working on revised versions of his Pooh drawings until shortly before his death. He remained devoted to his granddaughter Minette and her growing family, and greatly enjoyed their visits. Ernest Shepard died on 24 March 1976, at the age of ninety-six – the end of a long, happy and distinguished life and career.

CHAPTER 9

Shepard's Legacy

Over the nearly one hundred years since the publication of those first verses in 1924 there has been a constant pattern of new editions, versions and interpretations, but all based on the original four books. Well aware of the potential financial rewards, for a long time Milne and Shepard's literary agents, Curtis Brown, and publishers, Methuen and Dutton, had been encouraging, at times pleading, for more books. But Milne was adamant; he already felt hemmed in by Pooh, and distracted from what he saw as his 'serious' work as a playwright and poet, and had no inclination to continue. Shepard, too,

Cricket with Lottie the Otter.

was disinclined to encourage Milne; he could not see how he could fit in much more work, and in the period before and after the Second World War, both men were busy in other areas.

After the death of Shepard in 1976, periodic requests were made to the Milne and Shepard estates, principally from writers and artists, suggesting a wide variety of potential books and projects, all keen to benefit from association with Pooh. All these approaches were firmly rebuffed. Such matters were discussed at the meetings of the Pooh trustees (who represented the principal beneficiaries of Milne's estate), at which there was always (and still is) a pause for tea and honey sandwiches.

By the late 1990s, the then trustees of the Milne and Shepard estates came to the conclusion that the time was right to commission a sequel, one that would be appropriate and respectful to the original books. This all took much longer than had originally been anticipated, but in due course the author David Benedictus was commissioned to write a full-length sequel as one story, and Mark Burgess agreed to draw the accompanying illustrations in the style of Shepard. The principal issue for both writer and illustrator was to ensure a consistency of tone and language with the originals, without imitation or parody – a challenging task. Benedictus and Burgess worked long and hard to achieve the necessary balance, and the proof of the pudding was in the eating. *Return to the Hundred Acre Wood* was published in 2009 and was a great success.

Some years later, the Milne and Shepard estates considered commissioning a further sequel. After much deliberation, it was decided to commission four writers each to contribute a seasonally themed short story, which would together make up a full-length book. There was much discussion about who might be a good fit and how to maintain a consistent voice through all four stories. An integral part of these conversations was how the necessary illustrations could draw them together, using Shepard's originals as starting points and allowing Mark Burgess to weave the Shepard-inspired magic throughout the new book.

In due course, Kate Saunders, Brian Sibley, Paul Bright and Jeanne Willis were commissioned to write the four stories; probably the most challenging role was that of the editor, who had to work with each author to achieve an

Mark Burgess's illustrations for *Return to the Hundred Acre Wood*.

overall consistency of tone. Mark Burgess once more conjured with Shepard's original style to create the new illustrations. He even reworked the familiar endpapers to depict the seasons across the Hundred Acre Wood. And if for some the drawings occasionally veered towards the Disney cartoon versions of the 1960s, the overall impression was of a contemporary reworking of the Shepard style.

The resulting book, *The Best Bear in All the World*, with its separate Spring, Summer, Autumn and Winter stories – this time featuring a penguin, inspired by an early photograph of Milne, Christopher Robin and a toy penguin (see page 139) – was published in 2016 to coincide with the ninetieth anniversary of the first publication of *Winnie-the-Pooh*. To further commemorate the ninetieth birthdays of both Winnie-the-Pooh (first appearing in October 1926) and Her Majesty The Queen (born on 21 April the same year), a special short book was produced, written by Jane Riordan and with illustrations from Mark Burgess, entitled *Winnie-the-Pooh Meets the Queen*.

Mark Burgess's illustrations for *The Best Bear in All the World* (*above and opposite*).

And so the magic continues, and as the centenary of the Winnie-the-Pooh books' first publication approaches, the passage of time does not diminish their popularity or their appeal. Together, Milne and Shepard created a timeless world, with stories and images as resonant today as they ever were, and loved by children of all ages from generation to generation. Perhaps we should leave the last words to A. A. Milne:

When I am gone,
Let Shepard decorate my tomb,
And put (if there is room)
Two pictures on the stone:
Piglet from page a hundred and eleven,
And Pooh and Piglet walking (157) ...
And Peter, thinking that they are my own,
Will welcome me to Heaven.

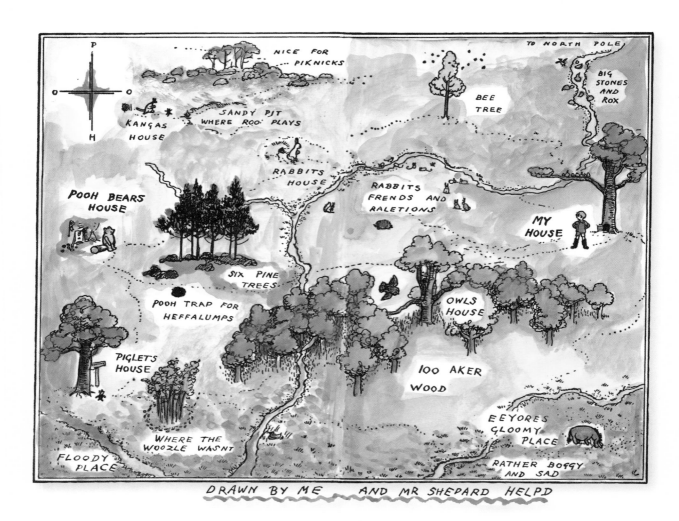

Endpapers for *Winnie-the-Pooh* (*above*) and *The Best Bear in All the World* (*opposite*).

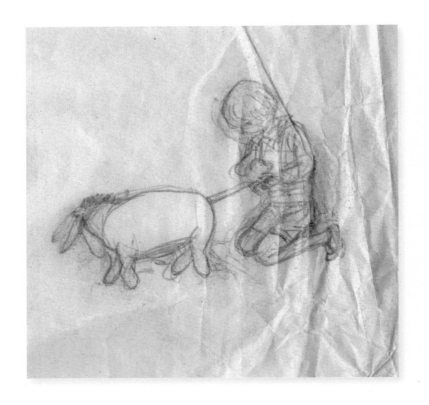

Acknowledgements

This book would not have been possible without the help and support of the Shepard family, and in particular Minette Shepard, E. H. Shepard's granddaughter, and her husband, Roger Hunt. They have been at all times generous, helpful and encouraging. They pointed me in the direction of many unseen illustrations and drawings, and Minette has kindly contributed the Foreword. Giles Hunt usefully located a cache of Shepard drawings in Tasmania, and drew these to my attention.

The staff of the E. H. Shepard Archive (part of the Archives & Special Collections at the University of Surrey) under the leadership of Caroline Rock, Director of Library and Learning Support Services, were consistently efficient, organised and helpful. Helen Roberts, Archives & Special Collections Manager, and Melanie Peart, Archivist (Collections Management), were particularly supportive, along with all the Archives & Special Collections team. Sharon Maxwell, now Archivist at the University of Reading, made a significant contribution at the earliest stage.

In the course of research for this book, we at last confirmed that E. H. Shepard's professional relationship with the Literary Agency of Spencer Curtis Brown commenced in 1920, and since that time Curtis Brown has represented first E. H. Shepard and later the Shepard estate on behalf of the Shepard Trustees. Stephanie Thwaites has provided consistent professional guidance and practical support, and Norah Perkins, Emma Bailey and Kate Cooper have all been enthusiastic, engaged and committed.

LOM Art published my previous book on E. H. Shepard and his experiences in the First World War, *Shepard's War*, and that harmonious and effective relationship has been sustained, with my editor, Fiona Slater, having been supportive from the start, giving sound criticism and prudent advice, which has made this a much better book than it would otherwise have been.

Egmont and Dutton, respectively UK and US publishers of the Pooh books, have generously allowed the use of published images from a variety of editions, and so particular thanks to Cally Poplak, Nicole Pearson, Natasha

Watkins and Kristina Kennedy from Egmont in the UK, and to Andrew Karre and Julie Strauss-Gabel from Dutton and also Michael Horn at Disney, in the USA. Mark Burgess, who illustrated both of the twenty-first-century Winnie-the-Pooh sequels, *The Return to the Hundred Acre Wood* and *The Best Bear in all the World*, has generously permitted the reproduction of drawings from these popular new books.

In addition to primary source materials, I have drawn on a number of existing publications – principal amongst these has been *The Work of E. H. Shepard* (Methuen, 1979) edited by Rawle Knox (stepson of Shepard's daughter Mary), *The Story of E. H. Shepard* (Jaydem Books, 2000) by Arthur Chandler, then University Archivist at the University of Surrey, *A. A. Milne* (Faber & Faber, 1990) and *The Brilliant Career of Winnie-the-Pooh* (Methuen 1992), both by Ann Thwaite, who kindly gave me advice and support. Shepard's own memoirs, *Drawn from Memory* (Methuen, 1957) and *Drawn from Life* (Methuen, 1961) have been the source of much detail about his early life. Contemporary illustrations of the Ashdown Forest were lent by Peter Freeland, and the photograph of Shepard's studio in Shamley Green was kindly provided by Bridget Eacott.

William Jensen, Robert Hunt and Nicholas Barlow as trustees of The Shepard Trust oversaw the project with wise guidance; my sister Sophie, a highly experienced writer herself, freely gave sound advice and suggestions; thanks are due to Rupert Hill and his fellow Pooh Trustees who were supportive of the project. And grateful thanks to Trish Henderson, without whom the organisation of my life would have collapsed.

My children, Rory, Marina and Freddy, have contributed in their own idiosyncratic ways, and as always, my long suffering wife, Arabee, has put up with the highs and lows as this book has progressed from glint in the eye to final proofs – and without her it would never have happened.

Any errors, omissions and failure to acknowledge sources accurately are entirely the sole responsibility of the author.

"The bees are getting
suspicious"

Picture Credits

Index